For C, B♭, E♭ & Bass Clef Instruments

MAIDEN VOYAGE

Play-Along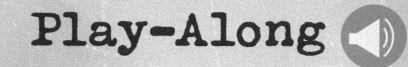

T0065881

To access online content visit:
www.halleonard.com/mylibrary

Enter Code
7111-6143-2467-9840

ISBN 978-1-4950-7472-1

HAL•LEONARD®
7777 W. BLUEMOUND RD. P.O. BOX 13819 MILWAUKEE, WI 53213

For more information on the Real Book series, including community forums, please visit
www.OfficialRealBook.com

Visit Hal Leonard Online at
www.halleonard.com

Contents

4

AUTUMN LEAVES

— Joseph Kosma/Johnny Mercer/Jacques Prevert

C Version

(Fast)

*TAG 2X TO END   FINE   AFTER SOLOS, D.S. AL FINE
                                      (PLAY PICKUPS) (TAKE REPEAT)

BLUE BOSSA

— Kenny Dorham

(MED. UP BOSSA)

C VERSION

PLAY HEAD TWICE IN/OUT
AFTER SOLOS, D.S. AL ✛ (PLAY PICKUP)

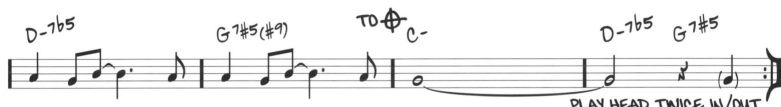

DOXY

— Sonny Rollins

C Version

(MED.)

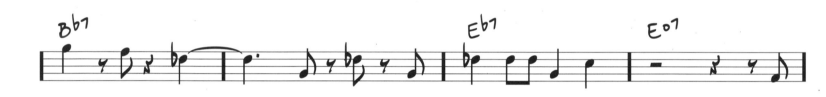

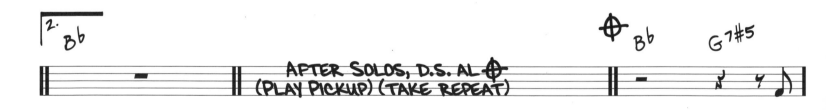

FOOTPRINTS

— WAYNE SHORTER

(JAZZ WALTZ)

C VERSION

REPEAT HEAD IN /OUT
TAG LAST 8 BARS 2X
VAMP INTRO 3X TO FINE

Maiden Voyage

- Herbie Hancock

C Version

Now's The Time

(Fast Blues)

— Charlie Parker

C Version

* OPTIONAL ON SOLOS

REPEAT HEAD IN/OUT
AFTER SOLOS, D.S. AL ⊕
(PLAY PICKUP)

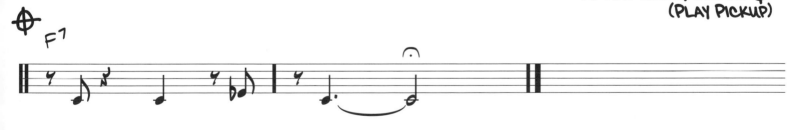

On Green Dolphin Street
(Med. Latin)
— Ned Washington/Bronislau Kaper
C Version

Summertime

– George Gershwin/DuBose & Dorothy Heyward/Ira Gershwin

(MED. BALLAD)

C Version

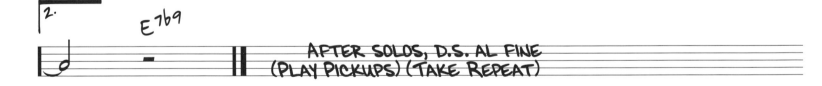

Tune Up

(FAST BOP)

— Miles Davis

C Version

FINE

(TAKE 1st ENDING ON SOLOS)

14

AUTUMN LEAVES

– Joseph Kosma/Johnny Mercer/Jacques Prevert

B♭ Version

*TAG 2X TO END   FINE   AFTER SOLOS, D.S. AL FINE
                                              (PLAY PICKUPS) (TAKE REPEAT)

Blue Bossa

— Kenny Dorham

(MED. UP BOSSA)

B♭ VERSION

PLAY HEAD TWICE IN/OUT
AFTER SOLOS, D.S. AL ⊕ (PLAY PICKUP)

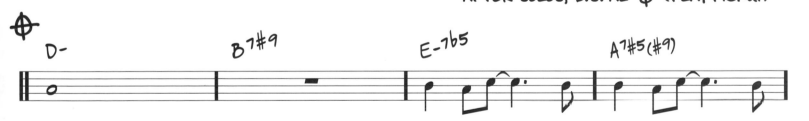

Doxy

— Sonny Rollins

(MED.)

Bb VERSION

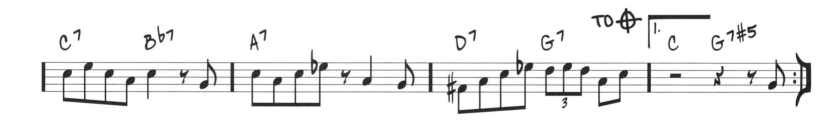

AFTER SOLOS, D.S. AL ⊕
(PLAY PICKUP) (TAKE REPEAT)

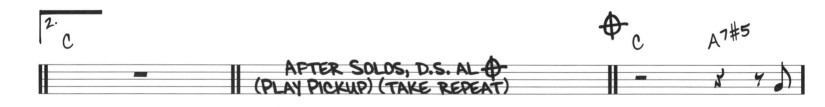

Footprints

(JAZZ WALTZ)
B♭ VERSION

— WAYNE SHORTER

REPEAT HEAD IN/OUT
TAG LAST 8 BARS 2X
VAMP INTRO 3X TO FINE

MAIDEN VOYAGE

— Herbie Hancock

Bb VERSION

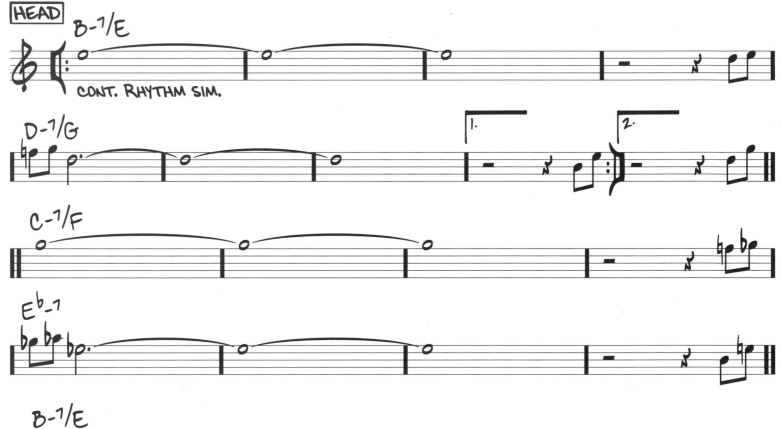

AFTER SOLOS, LAST HEAD,
PLAY INTRO 1X, END ON B-7/E

Now's The Time

— Charlie Parker

(Fast Blues)

Bb Version

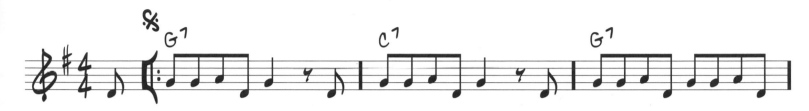

* Optional on Solos

Repeat Head In/Out
After Solos, D.S. Al ⊕
(Play Pickup)

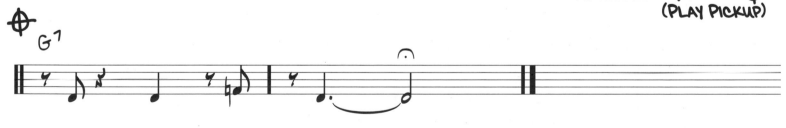

Satin Doll

— Duke Ellington

Summertime

— George Gershwin/DuBose & Dorothy Heyward/Ira Gershwin

(MED. BALLAD)

B♭ Version

FINE

AFTER SOLOS, D.S. AL FINE
(PLAY PICKUPS) (TAKE REPEAT)

Tune Up

(FAST BOP)

— Miles Davis

Bb VERSION

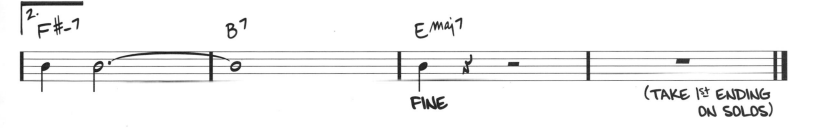

FINE

(TAKE 1st ENDING
ON SOLOS)

Autumn Leaves

— Joseph Kosma/Johnny Mercer/Jacques Prevert

Eb Version

(Fast)

*Tag 2x to end

FINE

After Solos, D.S. Al Fine
(Play Pickups) (Take Repeat)

Blue Bossa

— Kenny Dorham

DOXY

– Sonny Rollins

(MED.)

Eb Version

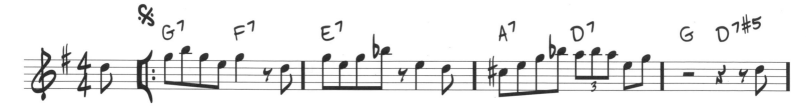

AFTER SOLOS, D.S. AL ⊕
(PLAY PICKUP) (TAKE REPEAT)

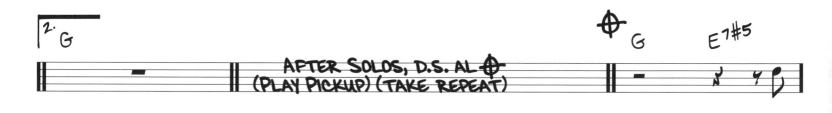

Footprints

— Wayne Shorter

MAIDEN VOYAGE

— Herbie Hancock

After solos, last head,
play intro 1x, end on F#-7/B

Now's The Time

(FAST BLUES)

— CHARLIE PARKER

Eb VERSION

* OPTIONAL ON SOLOS

REPEAT HEAD IN/OUT
AFTER SOLOS, D.S. AL ⊕
(PLAY PICKUP)

ON GREEN DOLPHIN STREET

(MED. LATIN)

— Ned Washington/Bronislau Kaper

Eb Version

FINE

AFTER SOLOS D.S. AL FINE
(TAKE REPEAT)

Satin Doll

— Duke Ellington

Summertime

- George Gershwin/DuBose & Dorothy Heyward/Ira Gershwin

Tune Up

- Miles Davis

Eb Version

(Fast Bop)

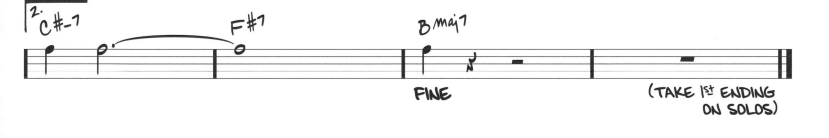

FINE

(TAKE 1st ENDING
ON SOLOS)

Autumn Leaves

Joseph Kosma/Johnny Mercer/Jacques Prevert

C Bass Version

*TAG 2X TO END   FINE   AFTER SOLOS, D.S. AL FINE
(PLAY PICKUPS) (TAKE REPEAT)

Blue Bossa

— Kenny Dorham

(MED. UP BOSSA)

C BASS VERSION

PLAY HEAD TWICE IN/OUT
AFTER SOLOS, D.S. AL ⊕ (PLAY PICKUP)

DOXY

— Sonny Rollins

(MED.)

C BASS VERSION

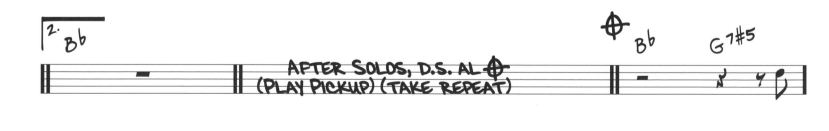

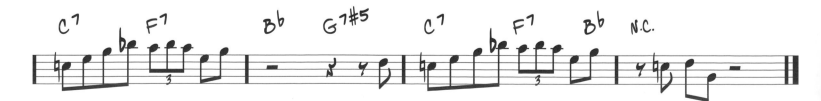

Footprints

— Wayne Shorter

REPEAT HEAD IN /OUT
TAG LAST 8 BARS 2X
VAMP INTRO 3X TO FINE

MAIDEN VOYAGE

— Herbie Hancock

C BASS VERSION

AFTER SOLOS, LAST HEAD,
PLAY INTRO IX, END ON A-7/D

Now's the Time

- Charlie Parker

C BASS VERSION

* OPTIONAL ON SOLOS

REPEAT HEAD IN/OUT
AFTER SOLOS, D.S. AL ⊕
(PLAY PICKUP)

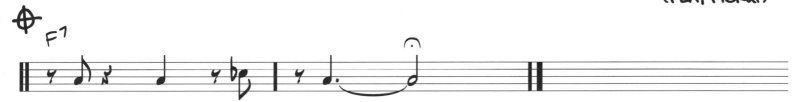

ON GREEN DOLPHIN STREET

(MED. LATIN)

— NED WASHINGTON/BRONISLAU KAPER

C BASS VERSION

FINE

AFTER SOLOS D.S. AL FINE
(TAKE REPEAT)

Satin Doll

— Duke Ellington

Summertime

Tune Up

– Miles Davis

(FAST BOP)

C BASS VERSION

FINE

(TAKE 1ST ENDING ON SOLOS)

The Best-Selling Jazz Book of All Time Is Now Legal!

The Real Books are the most popular jazz books of all time. Since the 1970s, musicians have trusted these volumes to get them through every gig, night after night. The problem is that the books were illegally produced and distributed, without any regard to copyright law, or royalties paid to the composers who created these musical masterpieces.

Hal Leonard is very proud to present the first legitimate and legal editions of these books ever produced. You won't even notice the difference, other than all the notorious errors being fixed: the covers and typeface look the same, the song lists are nearly identical, and the price for our edition is even cheaper than the originals!

Every conscientious musician will appreciate that these books are now produced accurately and ethically, benefitting the songwriters that we owe for some of the greatest tunes of all time!

VOLUME 1
00240221	C Edition	$45.00
00240224	B♭ Edition	$45.00
00240225	E♭ Edition	$45.00
00240226	Bass Clef Edition	$45.00
00286389	F Edition	$39.99
00240292	C Edition 6 x 9	$39.99
00240339	B♭ Edition 6 x 9	$39.99
00147792	Bass Clef Edition 6 x 9	$39.99
00200984	Online Backing Tracks: Selections	$45.00
00110604	Book/USB Flash Drive Backing Tracks Pack	$85.00
00110599	USB Flash Drive Only	$50.00

VOLUME 2
00240222	C Edition	$45.00
00240227	B♭ Edition	$45.00
00240228	E♭ Edition	$45.00
00240229	Bass Clef Edition	$45.00
00240293	C Edition 6 x 9	$39.99
00125900	B♭ Edition 6 x 9	$39.99
00125900	The Real Book – Mini Edition	$39.99
00204126	Backing Tracks on USB Flash Drive	$50.00
00204131	C Edition – USB Flash Drive Pack	$85.00

VOLUME 3
00240233	C Edition	$45.00
00240284	B♭ Edition	$45.00
00240285	E♭ Edition	$45.00
00240286	Bass Clef Edition	$45.00
00240338	C Edition 6 x 9	$39.99

VOLUME 4
00240296	C Edition	$45.00
00103348	B♭ Edition	$45.00
00103349	E♭ Edition	$45.00
00103350	Bass Clef Edition	$45.00

VOLUME 5
00240349	C Edition	$45.00
00175278	B♭ Edition	$45.00
00175279	E♭ Edition	$45.00

VOLUME 6
00240534	C Edition	$45.00
00223637	E♭ Edition	$45.00

Also available:
00154230	The Real Bebop Book	$34.99
00240264	The Real Blues Book	$39.99
00310910	The Real Bluegrass Book	$39.99
00240223	The Real Broadway Book	$39.99
00240440	The Trane Book	$25.00
00125426	The Real Country Book	$45.00
00269721	The Real Miles Davis Book C Edition	$29.99
00269723	The Real Miles Davis Book B♭ Edition	$29.99
00240355	The Real Dixieland Book C Edition	$39.99
00294853	The Real Dixieland Book E♭ Edition	$39.99
00122335	The Real Dixieland Book B♭ Edition	$39.99
00240235	The Duke Ellington Real Book	$25.00
00240268	The Real Jazz Solos Book	$39.99
00240348	The Real Latin Book C Edition	$39.99
00127107	The Real Latin Book B♭ Edition	$39.99
00120809	The Pat Metheny Real Book C Edition	$34.99
00252119	The Pat Metheny Real Book B♭ Edition	$29.99
00240358	The Charlie Parker Real Book C Edition	$25.00
00275997	The Charlie Parker Real Book E♭ Edition	$25.00
00118324	The Real Pop Book – Vol. 1	$39.99
00240331	The Bud Powell Real Book	$25.00
00240437	The Real R&B Book C Edition	$45.00
00276590	The Real R&B Book B♭ Edition	$45.00
00240313	The Real Rock Book	$39.99
00240323	The Real Rock Book – Vol. 2	$39.99
00240359	The Real Tab Book	$39.99
00240317	The Real Worship Book	$35.00

THE REAL CHRISTMAS BOOK
00240306	C Edition	$35.00
00240345	B♭ Edition	$35.00
00240346	E♭ Edition	$35.00
00240347	Bass Clef Edition	$35.00
00240431	A-G CD Backing Tracks	$24.99
00240432	H-M CD Backing Tracks	$24.99
00240433	N-Y CD Backing Tracks	$24.99

THE REAL VOCAL BOOK
00240230	Volume 1 High Voice	$40.00
00240307	Volume 1 Low Voice	$40.00
00240231	Volume 2 High Voice	$39.99
00240308	Volume 2 Low Voice	$39.99
00240391	Volume 3 High Voice	$39.99
00240392	Volume 3 Low Voice	$39.99
00118318	Volume 4 High Voice	$39.99
00118319	Volume 4 Low Voice	$39.99

Complete song lists online at www.halleonard.com

Prices, content, and availability subject to change without notice.

For use with all B-flat, E-flat, Bass Clef and C instruments, the Jazz Play-Along® Series is the ultimate learning tool for all jazz musicians. With musician-friendly lead sheets, melody cues, and other split-track audio choices included, these first-of-a-kind packages help you master improvisation while playing some of the greatest tunes of all time. FOR STUDY, each tune includes a split track with: melody cue with proper style and inflection • professional rhythm tracks • choruses for soloing • removable bass part • removable piano part. FOR PERFORMANCE, each tune also has: an additional full stereo accompaniment track (no melody) • additional choruses for soloing.

1A. MAIDEN VOYAGE/ALL BLUES
00843158 .... $22.99

1. DUKE ELLINGTON
00841644... $16.99

2. MILES DAVIS
00841645... $17.99

3. THE BLUES
00841646... $19.99

4. JAZZ BALLADS
00841691... $17.99

5. BEST OF BEBOP
00841689... $17.99

6. JAZZ CLASSICS WITH EASY CHANGES
00841690... $16.99

7. ESSENTIAL JAZZ STANDARDS
00843000... $17.99

8. ANTONIO CARLOS JOBIM AND THE ART OF THE BOSSA NOVA
00843001... $16.99

9. DIZZY GILLESPIE
00843002... $19.99

10. DISNEY CLASSICS
00843003... $16.99

12. ESSENTIAL JAZZ CLASSICS
00843005... $16.99

13. JOHN COLTRANE
00843006... $17.99

14. IRVING BERLIN
00843007... $16.99

15. RODGERS & HAMMERSTEIN
00843008... $16.99

16. COLE PORTER
00843009... $17.99

17. COUNT BASIE
00843010... $17.99

18. HAROLD ARLEN
00843011... $17.99

20. CHRISTMAS CAROLS
00843080... $16.99

21. RODGERS AND HART CLASSICS
00843014... $16.99

22. WAYNE SHORTER
00843015... $17.99

23. LATIN JAZZ
00843016... $19.99

24. EARLY JAZZ STANDARDS
00843017... $16.99

25. CHRISTMAS JAZZ
00843018... $17.99

26. CHARLIE PARKER
00843019... $16.99

27. GREAT JAZZ STANDARDS
00843020... $17.99

28. BIG BAND ERA
00843021... $17.99

29. LENNON AND MCCARTNEY
00843022... $24.99

30. BLUES' BEST
00843023... $16.99

31. JAZZ IN THREE
00843024... $16.99

32. BEST OF SWING
00843025... $17.99

33. SONNY ROLLINS
00843029... $16.99

34. ALL TIME STANDARDS
00843030... $17.99

35. BLUESY JAZZ
00843031... $17.99

36. HORACE SILVER
00843032... $19.99

37. BILL EVANS
00843033... $16.99

38. YULETIDE JAZZ
00843034... $16.99

39. "ALL THE THINGS YOU ARE" & MORE JEROME KERN SONGS
00843035... $19.99

40. BOSSA NOVA
00843036... $19.99

41. CLASSIC DUKE ELLINGTON
00843037... $16.99

42. GERRY MULLIGAN FAVORITES
00843038... $16.99

43. GERRY MULLIGAN CLASSICS
00843039... $19.99

45. GEORGE GERSHWIN
00103643... $24.99

47. CLASSIC JAZZ BALLADS
00843043... $17.99

48. BEBOP CLASSICS
00843044... $16.99

49. MILES DAVIS STANDARDS
00843045... $19.99

52. STEVIE WONDER
00843048... $17.99

53. RHYTHM CHANGES
00843049... $16.99

55. BENNY GOLSON
00843052... $19.99

56. "GEORGIA ON MY MIND" & OTHER SONGS BY HOAGY CARMICHAEL
00843056... $17.99

57. VINCE GUARALDI
00843057... $16.99

58. MORE LENNON AND MCCARTNEY
00843059... $17.99

59. SOUL JAZZ
00843060... $17.99

60. DEXTER GORDON
00843061... $16.99

61. MONGO SANTAMARIA
00843062... $16.99

62. JAZZ-ROCK FUSION
00843063... $19.99

63. CLASSICAL JAZZ
00843064... $16.99

64. TV TUNES
00843065... $16.99

65. SMOOTH JAZZ
00843066... $19.99

66. A CHARLIE BROWN CHRISTMAS
00843067... $16.99

67. CHICK COREA
00843068... $22.99

68. CHARLES MINGUS
00843069... $19.99

71. COLE PORTER CLASSICS
00843073... $16.99

72. CLASSIC JAZZ BALLADS
00843074... $16.99

73. JAZZ/BLUES
00843075... $16.99

74. BEST JAZZ CLASSICS
00843076... $16.99

75. PAUL DESMOND
00843077... $17.99

78. STEELY DAN
00843070... $19.99

79. MILES DAVIS CLASSICS
00843081... $16.99

80. JIMI HENDRIX
00843083... $17.99

83. ANDREW LLOYD WEBBER
00843104... $16.99

84. BOSSA NOVA CLASSICS
00843105... $17.99

85. MOTOWN HITS
00843109... $17.99

86. BENNY GOODMAN
00843110... $17.99

87. DIXIELAND
00843111... $16.99

90. **THELONIOUS MONK CLASSICS** 00841262 .... $16.99	125. **SAMMY NESTICO** 00843187 .... $16.99	160. **GEORGE SHEARING** 14041531 .... $16.99
91. **THELONIOUS MONK FAVORITES** 00841263 .... $17.99	126. **COUNT BASIE CLASSICS** 00843157 .... $16.99	161. **DAVE BRUBECK** 14041556 .... $16.99
92. **LEONARD BERNSTEIN** 00450134 .... $16.99	127. **CHUCK MANGIONE** 00843188 .... $19.99	162. **BIG CHRISTMAS COLLECTION** 00843221 .... $24.99
93. **DISNEY FAVORITES** 00843142 .... $16.99	128. **VOCAL STANDARDS (LOW VOICE)** 00843189 .... $16.99	163. **JOHN COLTRANE STANDARDS** 00843235 .... $16.99
94. **RAY** 00843143 .... $19.99	129. **VOCAL STANDARDS (HIGH VOICE)** 00843190 .... $16.99	164. **HERB ALPERT** 14041775 .... $19.99
95. **JAZZ AT THE LOUNGE** 00843144 .... $17.99	130. **VOCAL JAZZ (LOW VOICE)** 00843191 .... $16.99	165. **GEORGE BENSON** 00843240 .... $17.99
96. **LATIN JAZZ STANDARDS** 00843145 .... $16.99	131. **VOCAL JAZZ (HIGH VOICE)** 00843192 .... $16.99	166. **ORNETTE COLEMAN** 00843241 .... $16.99
97. **MAYBE I'M AMAZED*** 00843148 .... $16.99	132. **STAN GETZ ESSENTIALS** 00843193 .... $17.99	167. **JOHNNY MANDEL** 00103642 .... $16.99
98. **DAVE FRISHBERG** 00843149 .... $16.99	133. **STAN GETZ FAVORITES** 00843194 .... $16.99	168. **TADD DAMERON** 00103663 .... $16.99
99. **SWINGING STANDARDS** 00843150 .... $16.99	134. **NURSERY RHYMES*** 00843196 .... $17.99	169. **BEST JAZZ STANDARDS** 00109249 .... $24.99
100. **LOUIS ARMSTRONG** 00740423 .... $19.99	135. **JEFF BECK** 00843197 .... $16.99	170. **ULTIMATE JAZZ STANDARDS** 00109250 .... $24.99
101. **BUD POWELL** 00843152 .... $16.99	136. **NAT ADDERLEY** 00843198 .... $16.99	171. **RADIOHEAD** 00109305 .... $16.99
102. **JAZZ POP** 00843153 .... $19.99	137. **WES MONTGOMERY** 00843199 .... $16.99	172. **POP STANDARDS** 00111669 .... $16.99
103. **ON GREEN DOLPHIN STREET & OTHER JAZZ CLASSICS** 00843154 .... $16.99	138. **FREDDIE HUBBARD** 00843200 .... $16.99	174. **TIN PAN ALLEY** 00119125 .... $16.99
104. **ELTON JOHN** 00843155 .... $19.99	139. **JULIAN "CANNONBALL" ADDERLEY** 00843201 .... $16.99	175. **TANGO** 00119836 .... $16.99
105. **SOULFUL JAZZ** 00843151 .... $17.99	140. **JOE ZAWINUL** 00843202 .... $16.99	176. **JOHNNY MERCER** 00119838 .... $16.99
106. **SLO' JAZZ** 00843117 .... $16.99	141. **BILL EVANS STANDARDS** 00843156 .... $16.99	177. **THE II-V-I PROGRESSION** 00843239 .... $24.99
107. **MOTOWN CLASSICS** 00843116 .... $17.99	142. **CHARLIE PARKER GEMS** 00843222 .... $16.99	178. **JAZZ/FUNK** 00121902 .... $17.99
108. **JAZZ WALTZ** 00843159 .... $16.99	143. **JUST THE BLUES** 00843223 .... $16.99	179. **MODAL JAZZ** 00122273 .... $16.99
109. **OSCAR PETERSON** 00843160 .... $16.99	144. **LEE MORGAN** 00843229 .... $16.99	180. **MICHAEL JACKSON** 00122327 .... $17.99
110. **JUST STANDARDS** 00843161 .... $16.99	145. **COUNTRY STANDARDS** 00843230 .... $16.99	181. **BILLY JOEL** 00122329 .... $19.99
111. **COOL CHRISTMAS** 00843162 .... $16.99	146. **RAMSEY LEWIS** 00843231 .... $16.99	182. **"RHAPSODY IN BLUE" & 7 OTHER CLASSICAL-BASED JAZZ PIECES** 00116847 .... $16.99
112. **PAQUITO D'RIVERA – LATIN JAZZ*** 48020662 .... $16.99	147. **SAMBA** 00843232 .... $16.99	183. **SONDHEIM** 00126253 .... $16.99
113. **PAQUITO D'RIVERA – BRAZILIAN JAZZ*** 48020663 .... $19.99	148. **JOHN COLTRANE FAVORITES** 00843233 .... $16.99	184. **JIMMY SMITH** 00126943 .... $17.99
114. **MODERN JAZZ QUARTET FAVORITES** 00843163 .... $16.99	149. **JOHN COLTRANE – GIANT STEPS** 00843234 .... $16.99	185. **JAZZ FUSION** 00127558 .... $17.99
115. **THE SOUND OF MUSIC** 00843164 .... $16.99	150. **JAZZ IMPROV BASICS** 00843195 .... $19.99	186. **JOE PASS** 00128391 .... $16.99
116. **JACO PASTORIUS** 00843165 .... $17.99	151. **MODERN JAZZ QUARTET CLASSICS** 00843209 .... $16.99	187. **CHRISTMAS FAVORITES** 00128393 .... $16.99
117. **ANTONIO CARLOS JOBIM – MORE HITS** 00843166 .... $17.99	152. **J.J. JOHNSON** 00843210 .... $16.99	188. **PIAZZOLLA – 10 FAVORITE TUNES** 48023253 .... $16.99
118. **BIG JAZZ STANDARDS COLLECTION** 00843167 .... $27.50	153. **KENNY GARRETT** 00843212 .... $16.99	189. **JOHN LENNON** 00138678 .... $16.99
119. **JELLY ROLL MORTON** 00843168 .... $16.99	154. **HENRY MANCINI** 00843213 .... $17.99	
120. **J.S. BACH** 00843169 .... $17.99	155. **SMOOTH JAZZ CLASSICS** 00843215 .... $17.99	
121. **DJANGO REINHARDT** 00843170 .... $16.99	156. **THELONIOUS MONK – EARLY GEMS** 00843216 .... $16.99	
122. **PAUL SIMON** 00843182 .... $16.99	157. **HYMNS** 00843217 .... $16.99	
123. **BACHARACH & DAVID** 00843185 .... $16.99	158. **JAZZ COVERS ROCK** 00843219 .... $16.99	
124. **JAZZ-ROCK HORN HITS** 00843186 .... $16.99	159. **MOZART** 00843220 .... $16.99	

*These do not include split tracks.

JAZZ INSTRUCTION & IMPROVISATION

BOOKS FOR ALL INSTRUMENTS FROM HAL LEONARD

500 JAZZ LICKS
by Brent Vaartstra

This book aims to assist you on your journey to play jazz fluently. These short phrases and ideas we call "licks" will help you understand how to navigate the common chords and chord progressions you will encounter. Adding this vocabulary to your arsenal will send you down the right path and improve your jazz playing, regardless of your instrument.

00142384 .... $16.99

1001 JAZZ LICKS
by Jack Shneidman
Cherry Lane Music

This book presents 1,001 melodic gems played over dozens of the most important chord progressions heard in jazz. This is the ideal book for beginners seeking a well-organized, easy-to-follow encyclopedia of jazz vocabulary, as well as professionals who want to take their knowledge of the jazz language to new heights.

02500133 .... $17.99

THE BERKLEE BOOK OF JAZZ HARMONY
by Joe Mulholland & Tom Hojnacki

Learn jazz harmony, as taught at Berklee College of Music. This text provides a strong foundation in harmonic principles, supporting further study in jazz composition, arranging, and improvisation. It covers basic chord types and their tensions, with practical demonstrations of how they are used in characteristic jazz contexts and an accompanying recording that lets you hear how they can be applied.

00113755 Book/Online Audio $29.99

COMPREHENSIVE TECHNIQUE FOR JAZZ MUSICIANS
2ND EDITION
by Bert Ligon
Houston Publishing

An incredible presentation of the most practical exercises an aspiring jazz student could want. All are logically interwoven with fine "real world" examples from jazz to classical. This book is an essential anthology of technical, compositional, and theoretical exercises, with lots of musical examples.

00030455 .... $34.99

EAR TRAINING
by Keith Wyatt,
Carl Schroeder and Joe Elliott

Musicians Institute Press
Covers: basic pitch matching • singing major and minor scales • identifying intervals • transcribing melodies and rhythm • identifying chords and progressions • seventh chords and the blues • modal interchange, chromaticism, modulation • and more.

00695198 Book/Online Audio $29.99

EXERCISES AND ETUDES FOR THE JAZZ INSTRUMENTALIST
by J.J. Johnson

Designed as study material and playable by any instrument, these pieces run the gamut of the jazz experience, featuring common and uncommon time signatures and keys, and styles from ballads to funk. They are progressively graded so that both beginners and professionals will be challenged by the demands of this wonderful music.

00842018 Bass Clef Edition $19.99
00842042 Treble Clef Edition $16.95

HOW TO PLAY FROM A REAL BOOK
by Robert Rawlins

Explore, understand, and perform the songs in real books with the techniques in this book. Learn how to analyze the form and harmonic structure, insert an introduction, interpret the melody, improvise on the chords, construct bass lines, voice the chords, add substitutions, and more. It addresses many aspects of solo and small band performance that can improve your own playing and your understanding of what others are doing around you.

00312097 .... $19.99

JAZZ DUETS
ETUDES FOR PHRASING AND ARTICULATION
by Richard Lowell
Berklee Press

With these 27 duets in jazz and jazz-influenced styles, you will learn how to improve your ear, sense of timing, phrasing, and your facility in bringing theoretical principles into musical expression. Covers: jazz staccato & legato • scales, modes & harmonies • phrasing within and between measures • swing feel • and more.

00302151 .... $14.99

JAZZ THEORY & WORKBOOK
by Lilian Dericq & Étienne Guéreau

Designed for all instrumentalists, this book teaches how jazz standards are constructed. It is also a great resource for arrangers and composers seeking new writing tools. While some of the musical examples are pianistic, this book is not exclusively for keyboard players.

00159022 .... $19.99

JAZZ THEORY RESOURCES
by Bert Ligon
Houston Publishing, Inc.

This is a jazz theory text in two volumes. **Volume 1 includes**: review of basic theory • rhythm in jazz performance • triadic generalization • diatonic harmonic progressions and analysis • and more. **Volume 2 includes**: modes and modal frameworks • quartal harmony • pentatonic applications • coloring "outside" the lines and beyond • and more.

00030458 Volume 1 .... $39.99
00030459 Volume 2 .... $32.99

MODALOGY
SCALES, MODES & CHORDS: THE PRIMORDIAL BUILDING BLOCKS OF MUSIC
by Jeff Brent with Schell Barkley

Primarily a music theory reference, this book presents a unique perspective on the origins, interlocking aspects, and usage of the most common scales and modes in occidental music. Anyone wishing to seriously explore the realms of scales, modes, and their real-world functions will find the most important issues dealt with in meticulous detail within these pages.

00312274 .... $24.99

THE SOURCE
THE DICTIONARY OF CONTEMPORARY AND TRADITIONAL SCALES
by Steve Barta

This book serves as an informative guide for people who are looking for good, solid information regarding scales, chords, and how they work together. Includes over 20 different scales, each written in all 12 keys.

00240885 .... $19.99

Prices, contents & availability subject to change without notice.